30 Journeys in *30 Days*

By Allura Eshmun

Published by Eshmun Books
an imprint of Blue Light Journeys

Blue Light Journeys, LLC
PO Box 1925
Round Rock, Texas 78680
bluelightjourneyscompany@yahoo.com

Cover designed by FayeFaye Designs

ISBN-10:1-946666-04-1 paperback
ISBN-13: 978-1-946666-04-8 paperback
ISBN:978-1-946666-05-5 e-book
Library of Congress Control Number: 2017942660

Visit Allura Eshmun at http://alluraeshmun.com/

Contact Allura Eshmun at alluraeshmun@yahoo.com

https://www.instagram.com/alluraeshmun/

https://www.pinterest.com/alluraeshmun/

https://www.youtube.com/channel/UCDNFW293aCX6_ztW0mq

Books by Allura Eshmun

Allura's Mini Book of 30 Days Towards Peace

Allura Eshmun's 60 Days of Sayings

Acknowledgements

Special thank you to my husband and our children. Thank you, Momma, for being my number one fan. Thank you, Mr. Wilson and Mrs. Kinney for giving me your wonderful opinions and support. Thank you, Mrs. Colgrove for your words of encouragement.

HOW

How does one cry reading their own words? How does one write and not understand until months later what they write? How does one write and not know the power in their own words; typed by their own fingers? How does one write and touch many hearts and not have a clue about the power they have? How?

- Allura Eshmun 2016

CONTENTS

Dear Friend,

Each short story and poem in this book chronicles thirty different experiences over the last two years of my life. I believe each experience or lesson is a tiny part of my journey showing me who I am, and what I can create in my life.

I hope you enjoy reading *30 Journeys in 30 Days,* and are able to reflect on the lessons I share with you and how the stories may relate to your life or the lives of other people you know. My goal is to inspire conversations, questions and joy.

Sharing our stories help us learn about who we once were, who we are becoming and confirms we are *never* alone !

Enjoy!

Allura Eshmun
Experience, Understand,Love, Be

Believe and Create

Who do you believe yourself to be? A question that is part of my lesson today, and a lesson unfolding as I watch a television show called, *Super Soul Sunday* on OWN (Oprah Winfrey Network). During an interview, Ms. Winfrey's guest said, who do you believe yourself to be? Before I think of my own answer I sit still, because I've never thought of, heard of, or even answered this question for myself. I hear my own voice say out loud, "Who do I believe myself to be?" Wow, is what I think! Many thoughts come to my mind, but I have no answers; just a bunch of abstract thoughts.

Who do I believe myself to be? I ponder until my mind begins to categorize my answers.

I'm a mother. I'm a wife. A sister. A niece. A stay at home mom. As I get to the end of my list I realize

I am describing several identities or roles perceived by others.

Who do I believe myself to be?

Again I realized, I don't even think about myself. *Does it mean I don't believe in myself? I know, I need to believe in myself more and obviously I'm not believing enough or as I should.* So, I asked the question again. Who do I believe myself to be? Loving, strong, powerful are the first words coming to my mind, but again doesn't give a full description of what I am trying to say or what I am trying to create. Ah ha! Did you catch it ? I did. I'm awake now and that is a good slap in the face saying, "Allura you've got it now!" Wow! I need to write and think like a creator.

Who do I want to create myself to be?

Who do I want to create myself to be?

Who do I want to create myself to be?

Who do I want to believe and create myself to be?

I am a spiritual human being radiating love.

I am a woman with a gorgeous out-of-control Afro who is grateful. I am a person who heals through learning and teaching.

I am a woman who enjoys being present with her husband, children and family.

I am a woman who enjoys the simple moments, like the cool green grass cushioning my feet or watching a small humming bird fluttering from flower to flower and the smell of rain after a long hot summer day.

I am a woman who writes and speaks to the language of the soul.

I am a woman and old friend inspiring you through writing.

I am a woman who takes time to rejuvenate her Spirit with love.

I am a woman who loves *YOU* and wants you to hear this message.

Who do you believe and create yourself to be? Go out and create, with love in your heart, who you believe yourself to be?

Birthday

Today I woke up exhausted, because I went to bed late last night. I rolled over in the empty bed to face the clock. It read 9:00 a.m. I turned over in the opposite direction and heard the kids, my husband, and my Mom trying to talk softly, as if, I couldn't hear them. Their whispers said, "She's going to miss her birthday!" *I'm thinking, it's 9:00 a.m., how am I going to miss my birthday?* Then I remember, how every year Momma sings "Happy Birthday" at the time she gave birth to me. It is almost time for her to sing to me this morning. Right now, I really want to rest. So, I go back to sleep.

Fifteen minutes later, I woke up, got out of the bed and walked through the family room to the kitchen with my gown on, messy black satin hair bonnet and snot in my eyes. Momma and the kids are sitting at the table eating breakfast, and my husband is washing dishes. Everyone has a funny look on their face and I see a big box on the counter and a few pink and white envelopes. Their eyes tell me they are excited and hopeful I like what they've purchased for my birthday. I imagine — from their perspective— it's hard for them, because I rarely show excitement (they want to see) about gifts they purchase for me. I am told I carry a serene aura when I'm sad, nervous or excited. I sense they really want me to have a great birthday today.

My daughter says, "Mommy you should write a story about birthdays!" She is right and her statement triggered a question, "*What are birthdays*?" I think it's a day we celebrate the day we are born. It's a day we are grateful for the life we are given. It's the day we come into the world to learn how to create experiences. Birthdays are milestones. If you think about it — really— a birthday is what we create it to be and, we are more than just one day of celebrating. We are a multitude of experiences. Our lives are a series of accomplishments and failures telling us where we've been and hints about where we may be going.

Birthdays are really for the family. *Sometimes we need a reason to celebrate.* For me, it's another day.

Truth be told, I don't like to celebrate birthdays. I'd rather celebrate ordinary days. A day that doesn't get as much attention. Choosing an ordinary day and making it special, seems more fun. There are so many days on the calendar treated like it's not important. Each day is important. Each day links us to the future as we leave the past behind. We can't do without the non-birthday or other non-celebratory days. *So why not make those days special too?*

As I write trying to define birthdays for myself, I realize, I struggle with receiving. Every year before my birthday, I tell friends and family not to get me anything, because I don't want them stressing about getting me a gift. I block my blessings instead of allowing and learning to receive. Instead of saying, "Thank you!", my mind starts thinking; hoping the giver didn't go out of their way to get an expensive gift or spend too much time on an idea for a gift. I think for days about gift ideas for others I love. *Why do I want less for myself?*

Hours later, I received happy birthday phone calls from family, and friends; birthday hugs, money and cool gifts. A family friend wrote a song for me. I felt emotional and appreciative. The love was overwhelming. I am grateful.

Birthdays mean so many things. It's just a day. A day we chose to celebrate love and make life great together.

Happy Birthday!!

Sometimes

Sometimes, I feel like I'm trying to find love in endless tunnels of darkness. The only light guiding me is the white flame in the distance, that —I know— I will never be able to reach in this lifetime.

Sometimes, I stumble over huge hurdles, because I'm blindfolded, with fear I've created.

Sometimes, I am scared and nervous but, I take a step; even though I can't see the ground.

Sometimes, I pray for courage. I pray for wisdom. I pray for knowledge. I pray for grace then, I surrender.

Sometimes, I surrender all my fear with my hands up to the infinite blue above.

Sometimes, it's time to let go, in order to shine like the light in the distance.

Example

You know, I blamed and I complained for many years. I complained about — her! Sometimes, I was downright mad at her! It's normal to feel this way about someone. I'd often ask her, "Why won't you do this and why won't you do that?" Ugh!! As a teenager, I yearned for her answers to just about anything. During my 20's, I only wanted her to say what I wanted to hear. In my 30's, she watched me, and she let me do me. Now, I'm in my 40's, and the light is just beginning to flicker through the cracks of my stubborn skull. The veil of fog is lifting. Now, I see clearly her brilliance.

I always desired for her to just tell me what to do. Maybe she did, but, I didn't listen. I wanted her to say what I wanted to hear. Maybe she did, but again, I chose not to listen. Now, I understand while she watched me and let me live my life the way I wanted, I failed to watch and learn from her. All of these years, I've been a child having a tantrum and mad about what I *wanted*. Now I realize she gave me exactly, what I *needed*. She didn't have to speak the words. *She lived them*. I saw her be them. I accept her and cry tears of joy. Feel that! This discovery, my dear friend, is powerful.

I remember being a five-year-old little girl passing by my parents' bedroom and seeing her on her knees praying before she got into bed. She's my example; teaching me how to pray. I remember watching her slice and wrap fruit in tin foil, so she could eat it, as breakfast, while on her way to work. She's my example; teaching me how to eat healthy. I recall visiting her friends, during the holidays, to drop off goodies for their kids. She's my example; teaching me how to give. She lived compassion and passed it down to me.

She was a nurse at the hospital and at home; nursing us all back to health. Friends, folk, and family members came to our home to say, "Hi!" but, (now I know) they were really coming for healing. Amen! They came with issues and left refreshed and happier. On any given day, she'd pick up a co-worker who needed a ride. Catch it ? A car ride, a healing, or a helping hand; she's lifting others up along her way. She's my example.

She's not a fancy woman, but she fancied over

how my brother and I looked when we went to school; and, when we returned home to complete our homework, she made sure we crossed our T's and dotted our I's. When Daddy attended his fancy work dinners, she stood, in all of her flawlessness, by his side. A wife, a mother, a nurse, a friend; holding all of us together with love and putting herself last.

Momma's truth unfolded before me because I changed by allowing her loving examples into my experiences; and now, I understand. It reminds me of the song lyrics sung by James Ingram, "Everything must change and nothing stays the same. Mysteries unfold stories go untold. It's just the way of time. No one and nothing goes unchanged…" When you see a person's truth, it hits your heart. What an awesome feeling!

I am blessed. I am grateful; to be aware I am learning from my Momma! I hope I'm being a good example for my kids. I hope I am the example to them she is for me. I've learned from the best. I am still learning from the best.

Thank you Momma. I love you!

Rainbow

I am truly grateful,

but

please unbundle me!

Save me from the binds of my heart!

Unfold the mysteries, and make things true.

It's so cold walking in circles inside this pain.

Un-grip! Release me!

You say, *"I know who you are, and I've stood where you are now!"*

The rain stopped.

The Sun just arrived above the horizon, and now you tell me, *"It's just a game!"*

How could you watch me struggling to be?

For thousands of miles, I thirsted for only your love.

Then you say, "*Let yourself be free, to be a part of something new!*"

I'm trying, but, I am still blinded.

I want to see what's there, already.

Help me lift the veil, if I already have the tools.

Let go, so I can dance again on the rainbows.

You are not ready !

Music

It consumes me. I feel its vibration moving in all directions, as it surrounds my body. It touches my innermost emotions I don't understand and don't want anyone to know about. It tells my story as if it knows me or it brings me a story I don't yet know. It speaks to my heart and changes my energy. When I'm in its presence my head, shoulders, followed by my arms, hips and legs catch and hold onto — the rhythm. Finally, I'm dancing to the sound and *it* has taken full control over me; and I don't care. My worries fade away. It's the best feeling ever.

I'm talking about music and how it makes me feel.

Layla Hathaway is one of my favorite rhythm and blues singers. She has many songs I love. One of my favorite songs is called, "I'm Coming Back". Every time I hear this song, I understand, feel and hear many messages. *How can one song do that? Is it talking to my Spirit directly? Is it clearing my mind and secretly letting in messages I need decoded by my soul. It's like a drugless drug?* It NEVER gets old! *Have you ever heard a song and feel like the lyrics are telling your story?* Sometimes I stop, and talk to the radio, and say, "SANG that song!", like I'm witnessing a preachers sermon in church. Ha ha! It's like I want to interview the singer and ask them, if they wrote and sung the song only for me. Maybe, I'm being too much, or just overly happy to experience the joy of music.

It's amazing how music takes you back to the past and changes your current emotions at the same time. "Reminisce", by Mary J Blige is one of those songs. Every time I hear "Reminisce" I remember vividly listening to it in my headphones while sitting on an airplane, wearing my oversized college sweatshirt, and looking out the window in a daze. Colossal size tears dripped from my swollen red eyes, because I had so much fun with my boyfriend, who I just left back home way too many times. I was on my way back to college 1300 miles away from him. Reminisce use to be my happy and sad song to think about my boyfriend. The same boyfriend who is now my husband. Thank God!!

When my husband hears Easy E's lyrics, "*Cruising down the street in my Six-Four*". The thumps of the base and high pitch treble sounds gets him pumped up and ready to do his two step dance. My husband can remember, like yesterday, the place and time in his life when the song hit the popular music charts. The song also brings back memories of NWA and their ground-breaking style of music in the late 80's.

Years later when our children were in school, our daughter came home disappointed, because the kids in her elementary school class didn't know any rhythm and blues musical legends like Earth Wind and Fire or Chaka Kahn. She believes they make good music and she likes the artists. I smiled big on the inside because she appreciates (what I call) real music. While driving, our son sometimes nods his head in the back seat, to the CD playing and he sometimes stops to say, "Old school music is jamming!"

Music is a big part of our home life and we always blast music and dance. I can tell when the kids think too hard because they dance like, what I call, little rhythm-less nations; but when they enjoy the beat inside the sound they dance like they are free.

So when you are having a gloomy day or want to get pumped up, inspired or happy I hope you turn on your favorite song and lose yourself for a moment. Free yourself and enjoy the music!

Wound

Why do you go in with a knife and make a precision cut in the most intimate-deep-painful-oozing-ego-wound and serve it on a platter for me to watch? That wound coldly sits and continues to drip in its own blood; like a parasite newly separated from its host. Free and mad as hell, because the environment is new; unwelcoming to what it's acclimated to. Wet, rough and jagged around the edges; taking its last few breaths of darkness before it transitions back to light. I am finally free of my ego-wound, but I don't know how to heal. I don't know where to go or what to do. This feeling, *this experience*, is not written in text books. I'm watching my wound sit on the platter.

Lost.

Confused.

Why did you do this?

Are you mad…?

Maybe I'm not understanding?

My wound is struggling to heal, because you gave me no stitches. You left it open oozing puss onto the ground and now I am trying to figure out how to close it on my own. This is by far an early attempt to explain how I feel through my filter of experience, but I know you understand the energy in every word this story speaks.

I thought love is about being subtle, gentle and allowing time to do what it does. I have no ill intent in my heart. I am simply trying to understand. Is it the condition molding you into thinking taking away my comfortable ego-wound is okay? Or, is it just time for you and me to hear this in a different way, because the other ways have failed. Is it the shade of my outer beauty distracting you? *It is only a vessel.* Or is it my ego in overdrive? Do you think this is the best way to reach out? It's taken me a long time to sort this out and now I'm beginning to understand what happened on the day you sent ego away.

Send Judah first, because I am grateful and excited to be able to have a speck of awareness of this Spiritual path. But, it is the way in which you spoke a strange language that mildly haunts me.

Give me a little more light so I can see.

Don't leave me here while you stand closer to the light.

We are here together for a reason can you remember?

Vacation

Vacation is sleeping way past the alarm clock buzzer.

Vacation is staying in pajamas all day, and letting the crust in your eyes build up after several rounds of naps.

Vacation is waking up smiling with stinky breath, because there are no plans for the day.

Vacation is sitting on the comfy couch head-jerk-nodding, dozing and smelling the warm fresh peaceful summer air coming from the window.

Vacation is letting go of life's craziness and re-

learning to be lazy again.

Vacation is the time to temporarily escape all the crazy vampire people in our life.

Vacation is a time to have fun and to do whatever the hell we want.

Vacation is when I don't have to think, plan or rush to get somewhere on time.

Vacation is a time when we get a chance to break from our everyday routine to enjoy life in a different way.

When our kids began preschool my husband and I started planning yearly vacations. Our first trip was to Colorado. At that time we had no idea how the kids would travel 15-hours in a van, and we didn't know if our van could take us there comfortably. *How many potty stops will we have to make? Will I be able to drive half the trip without passing out from staring at the yellow and white lines on the road? Will the Fisher Price iXL's and movies keep the kids busy enough? Will my husband be, too tired to drive because he's worked all week?* I worried and had many questions, but we did it, and had a good time. The kids did well too, and the van gained 2000 miles on its engine in a week.

Five years have passed, and since then, we've

driven to see Minnie and Mickey Mouse in California and Florida, cruised to Mexico, flew to see our Nation's Capital and White House, saw the snow in the Windy City on Christmas, traveled throughout our state and had a couple of staycations. We are blessed to visit many places as a family.

Recently, my husband and I got the urge to go back to Colorado. On our first trip there we felt like Colorado is a place where we can retire. Colorado has everything we want in a state. Denver reminds us of every place we've lived together. Our second Colorado trip we didn't have our reliable roomy van. We had a smaller newer car to take us there. Our kids didn't need car seats, and upgraded to iPads on this trip. The kiddie toddler days are over. The kids know where we are going and how to get there. Now they tell us what places they want to visit once we get to our destination.

This time I didn't have all the questions. I just planed for the trip. I observed and focused on being present. I watched my family and learned how they know how to fully be on vacation; better than I do. Being present (focusing only on the moment I was experiencing) helped me to see my excessiveness. I spend too much time re-organizing, planning and insuring everyone's comfort when I'm supposed to be on vacation too. I learned, I loose myself in their happiness. It's not a bad thing, because I do have fun, but I need to loose myself in my own happiness sometimes. I've also learned vacations don't have to be far away and don't have to happen for long periods of time. Vacation can be simple, calm, quiet and peaceful moments. Every day, I try to find peaceful moments that feel like vacation. I do this simply by watching the birds from a window, focusing on my breathing, or thinking about what I am grateful for... These experiences take me to a happier, and a more peaceful place just like physically going on vacation.

Pushing the Boundaries

They push the boundaries and crush the boxes we created.

They crush the boxes one by one and faster than new ones can be made.

They tell us to get out of our minds and listen to them.

They are not ours to mold into a toy we can play with or toss around at our own will.

They are not meant to be contained inside a box we build around them.

They are gifts sent here to tell us, "Wake the hell up! Be present! Listen!"

I am sitting in a kindergarten classroom waiting to mentor a 5-year-old boy. As I sit and wait near his desk I watch him walk around the room. *His energy level is off the charts and it's only 8:00a.m.* The school bell rang fifteen minutes ago. He finally comes to his desk near me, but now I watch his little body drop to the ground and roll across the floor. He is not happy and having a temper tantrum like a 2-year-old. I guess he is upset about what another student said to him or he is learning how to express his anger or testing my patience, but it's work time. *When I arrived at 7:45a.m. his teacher made it clear we were to read and write, but he has other plans in this moment.* Minutes later he is up and off the floor and standing next to his teacher who stands at the front of the classroom. She's giving the other kids directions for the next hour while he persistently taps her hip, with his small fingers, trying to get her attention. He loudly and repeatedly asks several questions that she answers calmly and one by one like a pro. After being retold the goals for our mentoring session he comes over to sit next to me in the back of the classroom.

He won't look directly at my eyes when I speak to him. I'm trying to get him back on track reading or writing. My frustration is building, but I know he just wants attention, but he is pushing *my* boundaries. I'm trying to figure out— in my mind— how to put him in a box; how to contain him so there can be order and more focus on the goals for today. *Why is this adorable child so difficult?* I decided, to wait and remain calm, but I feel like screaming. I let him express himself. I let him lead. Within ten minutes he writes an amazing short story and he reads his above kindergarten level books. Before I left I wish him a good day and we do our secret hand shake.

Weeks later I sat before *my* teacher. Excited! Happy, (like a child*)* to be able to express myself to someone who partially understands my journey. I'd just become aware (on my own) of answers to questions I'd been seeking, for weeks. I kept repeating the same phrases and stories over and over; not listening to my teacher. He sat patiently and waited. Like an unfocused frog (*just like my five-year-old mentee*) I continued to repeat stories and answers like I was jumping randomly from thought to thought. Thankfully, my teacher continued being calm and more patient. I didn't have a tantrum on the floor because I am an adult, but showing similar behavior as the 5 year old boy. A cycle. Lessons repeat until we are ready to hear; until we are ready to see; and until we are ready to feel, accept and allow what is planned for us.

Kids have it. They feel it. And they know it. We just need to listen and be present with them to hear the messages. They'll continue to push the boundaries until we get it…

Parenting

Parenting is learning about yourself.

Parenting is giving tough love in order for another to grow safely.

Parenting is staying up late with the throw-up bucket and praying we don't have to use ibuprofen or acetaminophen.

Parenting is worrying all night about making the right decision.

Parenting is spoiling them when they need to be spoiled.

Parenting is setting boundaries when they need to be drawn.

Parenting is being a parent and not a friend.

Parenting is sacrificing yourself for the benefit of another.

Parenting is giving them all you thought you never had, but did.

Parenting is knowing when to step back and give them space to grow.

Parenting is providing a safe place so kids can learn to be who they are meant to be.

Parenting is hard and wonderful at the same time.

Parenting is watching yourself grow as your kids grow.

Parenting is holding your tongue and not saying, "I told you so!", when they make mistakes.

Parenting is recognizing the fine line of when to let go and when to hold on.

Parenting is watching them grow into brilliant adults.

Parenting is listening and letting them show you how it's done.

Parenting is saying, "I love you, you are important and you matter to me!"

Parenting is saying, "You are beautiful or handsome and I am so proud of you!"

Parenting is showing kids we are all human beings and we've made the same mistakes to!

Parenting is saying, "It's okay to feel how you feel."

Parenting is a blessing and gift.

Parenting is giving unconditional love.

Parenting is loving someone more than yourself.

Running

I look at people — and I wonder — then, I ask myself, "Why are they running?" Who are they running from? *Are you scared?* Are they running from themselves, and is it just a different version of what I do to myself?

It pains me to watch, because I am them. But to them we are separate. I struggle like you struggle. I hurt like you hurt. The energy that flows through me flows through you too.

I don't want to run. I've tried already. My feet and mind are tired. I'm at the edge of discovering more of what lies deep within me. I'm learning to sit within it and be myself.

It's hard living in a world where the contrasts are a joy to experience, but difficult, because we put each other in cruel categories like we are grossly different. We have failed to pull back the layers of truth and to see we are one in the same.

Hard to Be Human

It's hard being human sometimes; when you try to describe the power of love, but language fails and cannot *fully* explain what it is.

It's hard being human sometimes; when your child asks you how the clouds were created and no mathematical equation or bible story can sufficiently answer how they got there.

It's hard being human sometimes; when we are right and wrong in the same moment of time and through several perspectives.

It's hard being human sometimes; not understanding fear is an illusion we've created and we have the power to turn it back into love.

It's hard being human sometimes; when you have a story and I have a story and both are opposite experiences, but both stories are correct.

It's hard being human sometimes; understanding why people shoot and kill in one part of the world and how there is peace across the waters in another part of the world and the energy that flows through us is all the same.

It's hard being human sometimes; when I pray hard for others I don't know well and they judge me based on my exterior and not the love I radiate.

It's hard being human sometimes; understanding when an answer is yes, but feels like no and all other options in between are correct too.

It's hard being human sometimes; when I see a child who is screaming for attention and I can only give a two second hug or high five.

It's hard being human sometimes; when I know a child wants to be free and all I can do is watch and pray they find the way on their journey.

It's hard to be human sometimes; when you are supposed to take care of yourself first, but take care of others first instead of yourself.

It's hard being human sometimes; when we learn to free our self from ego, but must be grateful for it, because ego can save our life.

It's hard being human sometimes; when we know

we need to focus on what we love, and we spend our lives doing what we hate, because we believe we won't make enough money doing what we love.

It's hard being human sometimes; when you are concerned, but don't want to be too concerned to point of worry.

It's hard being human sometimes; when you learn you only have yourself to blame for not living a better life.

It's hard to be human.

Be

I don't know when, or at what point in my journey, I became aware I checked off milestones on the *Life Check List*.

- ✓ Go to church
- ✓ Honor thy mother and father
- ✓ Get good grades in school to get into a good college
- ✓ Graduate from college
- ✓ A nice place to live and a money making career
- ✓ No pregnancies before marriage
- ✓ Marry a God-fearing man
- ✓ Buy a house
- ✓ Have kids
- ✓ Be happy

By the time I approached the end of the *Life Check List* I felt lost, because I realized there is not a certain way to live. I felt stuck and began questioning, trying to figure out what else to do with my life. I remembered observing others in the same situation who beat themselves up, because they were heavily criticized for completing the *Life Check List* out of order. I learned life cannot be controlled or contained by *only* obeying a list of commandments no matter the order. Following a check list is not a road map to life fulfillment. *It may be a compass guiding us to where we think we want to go.* When we force a certain way to be with mental deadlines and over the top expectations of ourselves, others and what we see others do is when the veil of life gets hazy. This way of thinking causes life to fall apart, because we put all our energy into a list of expectations. We are conditioned to want or feel the need to have a certain way to be and it's okay. A Yiddish proverb says, "When we plan, God laughs!" Translation: we are on God's time. We can plan if we want to, but God has the final say.

Even though I know the truth I still have moments when my *ego* shows me fear. I start stressing about what others, who follow similar *Life Check Lists*, will say. Thankfully love, faith, wisdom and courage help me stay balanced, in my life. I remind myself to remember my spiritual journey is mine and the path I take, on my own time, in my own way. To refocus, I ask myself, what makes me happy? What brings me joy? What will I do for me? How can I consistently be in alignment with my own human Spirit, because that is truly being?

The *Life Check List* is an illusion. *There is no certain way to be, but me.*

When I write, over and over and over, I dare to take a step off the ledge and fly like a baby bird who for the first time leaves the comforts of the nest. There is no right or wrong, good or bad, way to live as long as we *don't* intentionally hurt each other.

It's about how you flow with life. Life is about how you row your boat gently down the stream. Merrily, I hope!

Blind

I'm blinded and now I'm searching. I'm searching for a runway to land this plane, but the turbulence up here is so intense I can't do it yet. My view is real cloudy, and I have no map or flight destination. I am freely flying in open space and the wind is guiding me to where I need to go. I keep wondering where I will land or if I will land and how I will land?

I'm searching for my belief system, because I don't fit into the blinding pre-existing conditions. Some conditions look really good, but are not for me. It's like passing by a store front window, but that's all I'm doing; passing through the experience not settling in or finding out.

As I'm flying I realize my belief flows through me. I can't land on it or search for it. I just know it is there for me when I need it. The clouds parted some, the flight steadied, but this altitude and flight pattern is temporary; sustaining me, until I get to the next view.

A philosophy can't box me.

A mindset can't control me.

I fly in the wind. Guess I'll never land.

Enough

I always wondered when the story about him would surface.

On Friday every one came home from their busy day — with a story to tell. After listening to each story, and eating dinner, the kids showered, and got into bed. Momma laid down in the guest room. My husband and I sat down and watched a television program together. The show made us laugh hysterically. The kind of laughing you do when you sweat a little, grab your stomach and hold your head because it hurts to laugh. *An enjoyable moment needed after a long day.*

As we settled down and started watching more TV

my husband says, "Do you ever feel like you can't get enough of something?" I said, "Yes! I can't get enough of Sunday afternoons when we are all relaxing. I can't get enough of the smell of the damp earthy air blowing through the window. The smell of earth's aroma calms me and helps my body relax. I can't get enough of when we go on vacation and have a great time; sharing, learning, being ourselves and not strapped to our everyday routine. I can't get enough time by myself with no distractions! I can never get enough of walking outside near water!" My husband adjusts his body on the floor where we are sitting. He looks up at me then says in the clearest calmest tender voice, "I can't get enough of you!" Then he continued watching TV.

He does not know the weight of his words. Those words are screaming at me and trying to sink into my mind and spirit. WOW! Did he just say, "I can't get enough of you?" My ego says, "Say something bigger and better than what he just said…" but, he does not require a response. It just is…

Why are the words resonating within me so deeply? I don't know how to react or act? Who are you? You are showing me part of you I am trying to understand. You seem unaware of the value of the statement — I can't get enough of you! I feel underserving. The words reach the pureness of my

42

heart and coats me with light, forcing me to accept truth. Maybe, I'm being too much.

I.

Love.

My husband.

There is an ease we have in the present moment. The ease flows through us bonding us like glue. Through the years we've learned to allow each other to be. We know how to pull each other up when one of us is down. We encourage each other to have no fears about being who we are and who we want to create ourselves to be.

I can't get enough of you!

The simplest words bring tears to my eyes.

I'm sitting in the energy of it all. Trying to allow it to surround me. I am grateful.

When you can't get enough of something. It's like being five years old again and feeling the rush of gliding down a playground slide over and over again. It's like an nine year old cannon ball diving into a swimming pool over and over until exhausted. It's like not being able to just eat one piece of chocolate, because the flavor is so addictive and enticing. It's like wanting to play a favorite song over and over again, because it gives a feeling of oneness or joy . It's loving someone hard, deep and enjoying losing yourself because you are happier being ONE with them.

I can't get enough of you is a gift of words I will treasure.

I can't get enough of you?! I'm still trying to allow and accept those words.

In the Clouds

Has my head been in the clouds all this time? Wanting to be walking in wakefulness, but really walking aimlessly through life disconnected from reality.

Knowing, but not knowing.

Wanting, but not living.

Clinging onto the life's comforts that take me nowhere.

Refusing to feel and accept being numb.

Lost in empty space only hearing echoes of time passing…

Fear has me traveling for days in a maze searching for answers.

I'm stuck in the dream of thought, that seems so cruel.

Show me the tools of grace, wisdom, courage and peace.

Show me how to use love as my light in the darkness.

Help me get out of here, because I can't see my light.

Perfect

    I see you wearing the red lipstick — in the video moving your hips — looking all confused with a smile. I see you news anchor; trying to stay inside your suit. Your body is pushing on the seams of your size eight suit when a more comfortable size is probably twelve. Silicon breast, butt and chin. Changing our bodies to be tucked, sucked and pulled in. "Baby age twenty-five came and gone!" Age forty-five approached you so gracefully. I hear and see you news reporter trying to maintain a lifeless monotone robotic voice. There is no certain way to speak, but, to speak. I see you reality show judges trying to force those singers into a one size fits all mold. You've forced these singers into believing they'll only make it based on how they look; hair fried, dyed and laid to the side and those eyebrows arched and penciled in with heavy black marker. Your eyebrows screamed at me before I could get to know you. *It's only a distraction.* There are even coaches to keep up this façade or what we think perfection is... Why do we have a distorted sense of perfection? *Perfection can't be forced. Only allowed.* It isn't necessary to try so hard. But we do...

Are we playing a role, in a movie, in our head, we secretly hope to get an academy award for, or is it we don't want to do the work on our inner-self? *Why are we addicted to a false sense of perfection?* Blame it on Momma, or Daddy, or society, or conditioning, or factors outside our self. Excuses are all the same. But it's you. Yes you! Now don't trip, because I called you out, and don't get it twisted, because I am just like you, and we all need each other so no one can escape this human experience. So now we got EGO checked back into its prison cell on block 666 let's continue.

Let me remind you how Perfect you are already! You woke up this morning and you are breathing. PERFECT!

When you think about the things you don't want to do today, and tomorrow and your child calls your name 3 trillion times; trying to knock you out of a self-induced coma of your thoughts, to be present to life. PERFECT!

When you are trying to figure out how to rob Peter to pay Paul and a $65 check comes in the mail you did not expect. Amen. PERFECT!

When you've searched for a job for months and you just want to work and an inner voice says, "Don't give up, keep trying, because something bigger and better is on its way!" PERFCT!

When you've done everything in your being to help your hard headed child. It seems nothing you say sinks in their head, because they think, *they know* everything. Then you remember, you've traveled the same road and can see your mistakes in them, *clearly*! You feel like giving up on them, but your love for them is too strong to give up. PERFECT!

When your medical deductible is so ridiculously high it makes more financial sense not to have surgery. You feel violated by the healthcare system and insurance company. You are only trying to do the right thing. The next day comes and you still don't know how you are going pay for the surgery, but you have an internal unwavering faith telling you it's going to be alright, because you are not alone and you have your faith to stand on... PERFECT!

When you are driving and you know good and well you should have filled up your gas tank 40 miles ago and the gas light is red and you literally roll into a gas station right in front of the pump with a gas tank completely empty, but you made it. PERFECT!

When you see politicians who only work for themselves and not for those they serve. You finally decide to do something about it, because you refuse to depend on somebody else to control your happiness. PERFECT!

Stop and take a look at the trees, the animals and each other. They are all our reminders of who we are. Can you see and feel the beauty around and within ? Take a look, it really is perfect!

I want you to know, you are perfect, mistakes and all. So lift your head up and be proud. We are perfect. Let the church say Amen. Ha ha ... ! PERFECT!!

Super Heroes

It's that time of year again when the temperature outside cools giving us a break from the three digit degree days of summer. The sun goes down earlier than months before. The grass and trees begin transitioning from green to yellow to orange to brown. We remember to go deep in our closets to pull out our long sleeve shirts and light sweaters; to prepare for the cool days ahead. The kids start talking about Halloween, because they see the neon orange "Get Your Costume Here" signs in store windows prompting them to talk about what they are going to be on Halloween. I'm sure there will be countless superhero costumes. Later, I think more about super heroes because my husband is watching Daredevil; a Marvel Comics character and a television show. Daredevil is a vigilante/superhero who tries to keep the bad guys from destroying his city. Like a kid trying, to decide what costume to pick, I thought, if I were a super hero who would I be or what would my powers be? I would love to be able to speak all languages on our planet. I would love to travel to Shanghai, Brazil, India or Senegal and speak the languages with ease and with no preparation. Can you imagine being able to speak all the languages of every living form of the world?

I just had a moment while sitting here in my super hero wishing mode. We are all blessed with super hero powers. It's just not what we think, because sometimes life imitates art and we only believe what we see, and have no faith in the unseen. I thought about all the people who are close to me, those who have supported me and taught me lessons. They are my super hero survival team.

My husband is the Grounder. When I am in my obsessive mode his words are the reference point which helps keep me present, encouraging me to just be me. My daughter is the Imaginer. She constantly teachers me to be a kid again and to use my imagination to create what I want in my life. My son is the Compassionate. He never lets me forget to love and be kind to others. My brother is the Traveler. He's teaches me to expand my mind and go places outside of my element to try new things. My friend Jack is the Agape and he is able to give over the top amounts of love and reminds me when life gets tough love never fails. David is the Visionary and is able to see beyond the present and he tells me stories to help me stay focused on journey. My friend Iesha is the Genuine Warrior. She sees phony a mile away and if I am not being true to myself she is the first one to tell me to snap the hell out of it and keep it real. Dun is the Energy Manipulator. He teaches me how to maintain a positive energy flow though exercise, breathing and how to use its benefits. Tameka is the Easy Going. She reminds me to chill, keep it simple and relax a bit. There are many others you could call them the smiler, the laugher, the giver, the hugger, the prayer warrior. They all teach and bring me joy.

All these people in my life are Super Heroes and they share their gifts with me constantly. They all help me be the best me. Amazing! Talk about an aha moments...and, "You know what?" I am a Super Hero too! I am the Inspirer. I inspire and teach people, through writing, to be their true self. I see the best in people. I'm blessed with the ability to help guide them to turn in their inner light so the world can see Gods gifts come out of the darkness.

Stop

stop! Stop it! STOP IT!

Stop looking!

Stop searching!

Stop trying to find it or figure it out!

Stop believing your ego and your condition. They are illusions.

Stop over analyzing. You! Yes, YOU!

You are it. You are right where you should be and

the time is now, to love yourself.

Love the you, you already are and what you have created yourself to be.

Inhale these words, feelings and their meanings to unfold within your heart.

You are powerful.

You are enough.

You are amazing.

You are worthy.

You are deserving.

You are important.

You matter.

You are wonderful.

You are capable of receiving and giving love.

You are a phenomenal and infinite being.

Allura Eshmun

The world is at your doorstep. Take a step, then leap, then run and let the wind of peace guide you.

It may seem hard at first, but the love in you will be all the light you need to find your way!

You are not alone and never will be.

Know

Everything is everything

what we *do* know, we *don't* know

what we *don't* know, we *do* know

we are infinite and minute

death is life and life is death

love keeps balance

What is a Name?

Vibration

of feelings driving thoughts;

producing intricate sounds

downloading and translating into patterns of letters

forming a word

Energy

shaking up emotions

Noise

feeling rough or comforting

make us laugh or give us no sensations at all

Strong

enough to bring life into fear

light enough to shift us into the beauty of love

Imprints

of spaces we can go back to reminding us of
where we've been and where we want to go

Separation

putting us inside a

plethora of labeled boxes

Allura Eshmun

Titles

given based on conditions

we chose or are born into

Answers

helping us find our way

Fun

expressing the spirit of who we are

Mean everything and nothing

Words we give power to

Names are an illusion

Easter

Weeks before the big day Momma buys me a new pink dress and my brother a new gray suit. On Friday she washes my hair, greases my scalp, and plaits my hair. Saturday night, I sit in a chair between the stove and the sink to get my hair pressed. Once the hot comb surrounds each strand, my hair magically changes from nappy to straight. After all my hair is flattened and silky she adds gigantic pink sponge rollers. When she finishes, I can go to play in my room. On the way there, I see Daddy. He's in the bathroom which is across the hall from my bedroom. He is looking at his white chalky pasted chin in the mirror. Ewww!! Daddy has put stinky Magic Shave on his face again. I pinch my nose, walk to my room a little faster to evade the smell while he finishes shaving his face!

The next day on Easter morning, I watch everyone get ready to go to church. Momma is putting on make-up which is something I don't watch her do often. I have on my pretty white slip with lace edges, my good socks and dress shoes, because Momma doesn't want me getting my dress wrinkle or dirty, before we get to church. I don't know what my brother is doing in his room, but I'm excited, because Easter Sunday is the day we do a little extra to make sure we look our best and I get to open my Easter basket.

Momma helps me put on my dress and tells my brother to put on his shoes so we can go to church. I hear Daddy open the creaky front door then I hear him turn on the loud Ford Fairmont station wagon. We are all looking good; new clothes, picked out afros and fancy hair styles. We are going to church together. Momma is off from working at the hospital today and Daddy doesn't have any sales paper to fill out for work.

Precious childhood memories feel like yesterday.

I am so grateful for all the experiences I've shared with my family. Times change and I've watched and now see the world through a different filter of experience. The experiences are equal to watching a silent movie with me as narrator. It goes a little something like this…

It's Easter Sunday and even though it's unspoken among the fellowship every one entering church today will be in their finest clothes. The sisters of the church walk in wearing pastel dresses with matching hat, high-heeled shoes and purse. They spent 6 to 8 hours at the hair salon, in the kitchen. The brothers also wear their finest pastel or dark blue suits, with matching polished gator shoes, socks and some with matching fedora or panama styled hat. They waited for hours at the barbershop to get that perfect sharply edged up forehead line from the barber yesterday. The teenagers walk behind their families, disconnected from the present moment and in a daze, not wanting to be at church, but there because their Mom forced them to attend and dress up. This means girls dresses need to be loose and come down closer to the knee and the boys must pull their pants up to the waist, wear a tie and no sneakers, only dress shoes. Grandma already warned, "No texting, no pictures or getting on Instagram or Snapchat in Gods house. Turn off your cell phone!"

Walking into the main sanctuary everyone greets each other with smiles and whispered hello's, but inside our minds, we are really checking out (judging) who has on what and which CEO has come to church this time. The letters CEO is an acronym for 'Christmas Easter Only' and describes members who only go to church two times a year. Some female facial expressions say, "Oh! No, she didn't look at me and my kids that way and why are they wearing jeans and sneakers in the house of the Lord!" The brothers watch and nod to each other with their unspoken language. By the looks on his face Pastor is nervous about his sermon. The deacons are ready to give praise. The choir is ready to march down the aisle to finally sing the new songs they've been practicing for months. An hour later we sit in the pews waiting for announcements to end so Pastor can hurry up and preach. The sisters worry about cooking the rest of dinner and praying pastor will not preach pass 1:30pm. A few brothers glance at their watches because they can't wait to see the basketball game at 2pm. We all look good, but our clothes start to get hot and uncomfortable as we sit almost shoulder to shoulder. One sister just leaned forward to scratch her panty hose and some ladies are sliding off their stilettos to rest their sore swollen feet. It hurts to look good. The smaller kids are restless because they don't normally sit in the sanctuary this long and can't wait to sing their Easter song. All this and church is not even half way through... Together we are all dedicated to praising

Jesus. Hallelujah!

I could go on and on and add more details, but I think, what I've written paints a familiar picture. I still marvel at the great lengths we go through to polish our physical appearance, but have we forgotten the meaning of Easter? Have we forgotten the purpose of church? Have we distorted the purpose of religion? Are we just going through the motions because it's a habit we think will automatically make us good people and we think going to church is a certain way to be good? Have we lost our truth?

Easter is a celebration of eternal life. The resurrection of Jesus Christ is the beginning of our awakening and understanding that we are eternal just like him. Our Spirit never dies. Jesus, a healer and teacher awakened and provided a loving space for us to learn about ourselves. This peaceful eternal space within us is our part of God.

Jesus's story tells us how infinite we are and how to focus on our self and love who we are within. He taught us how to heal each other through love. He taught us to how to feed each other, give to each other, help each other. He's taught us how to take care of one another. He taught us how we are one and connected. He showed us how to love our spirit and humanness.

So, what's the purpose of going to church? Church is any sacred space we go to heal our self with others who seek the same within themselves. We go to learn how to get back into alignment with our loving self. It's the place where we learn over and over again how to allow life as it comes in each moment. We learn how to allow our humanness; to learn we are not alone and are part of something bigger than ourselves. It's a place we learn how to allow love again. We learn together how to be kind, compassionate, forgiving and give unconditional love to ourselves and each other. It's a place to meet others who also believe. We are not required to go stand or sit inside a building for an hour or two every Sunday morning to discover this truth and live this truth.

What's the purpose of religion? Religion is a practice we use to experience and understand our spirit. Religion is a guide we use to understand our spiritual purpose. Sometimes this includes exercising certain rituals to help us feel the spirit within us.

What does Easter mean to you? When you are with your family discuss the importance of church and what it means to you? Do you think we have lost the meaning of Easter and Church?

Pieces

If feels like we do everything with love in our heart and we still judge, as if, we are broken and need to be fixed.

We question, "Did I do enough?"

YES!

We give life to several outcomes happening only in our mind.

IT'S ONLY AN ILLUSION!

It feels like someone threw a million pieces of life in the air.

Seconds pass between each piece we watch slowly crashing to the ground one by one.

Now the task is to figure out how to get life back in our order.

Have you temporarily lost faith within yourself?

No one can help you, but you.

No one can be you, but you.

What will you do?

Will you take a step even when you can't see the ground ahead?

How will you turn this opportunity into a fresh new start?

The greatness lies within you!

LOVE!

Take a step and fully release the old so your blessings can take their rightful place.

Holidays

In my house, the fragrant smelling aroma of cinnamon and nutmeg, mixed in with the scent strawberries and peaches permeating through the air, bring back welcomed memories of my childhood home. At my grandmothers house it's the smell of butter, sage, celery and onion cooking on the stove. In my parents house it's the smell of a pine tree, feelings of love, and comfort. The holiday season is an exciting time.

Together, life events and returning home for the holidays is like a baseball game. We run through all the bases of life returning to home plate. Each base represents milestones we've created, and helped us understand more about who we are. We are all running through our bases at different speeds. Humanity shares the same game; each version just looks different. During the holiday season my mind travels to the past experiences and moves to the present ones. All experiences, feelings and thoughts give me a bigger perspective of where my journey started.

Spending time with some of my family members I only get to see once a year is a good thing. The truth is I really don't want to see them, but it's great to know they are alive and okay. Being around certain family members makes me question if a time machine dropped me off and it's really the 1960's and not the 21st century. Some family members AIN'T never changed and NOT NEVER going to! Yes, in my 'sistah girl' voice, I said, "Not never!" When my family finally gets together it's like watching a movie. Each family member is a character and most of them deserves an Academy Award for best dramatic actor or actress.

Everyone's got a character in their family they love and hate at the same time. You love them because they are always themselves and you hate them, because they love to go around the room telling people's truth or their version of it.

There are the alpha's. Poppa (grandfather) and Mawh Mawh (grandmother) who are in charge of keeping everybody together. Even the family members who can't stand each other. When the alpha speaks everyone listens.

Uncle Willis always has a barrel of Mickeys Beer or scotch in his hand. Uncle W. is a magician too. He can trip, fall and land on his back with a cup in his hand and never spill a drop of alcohol. His breathe always reeks booze and he loves telling stories about everybody else. So we sit with popcorn like we are watching a movie while he tells his story.

Uncle Ulysses never comes out of the back room at grandmothers house and never ever ever shows up to family functions. When he showed up this year everybody stopped, and their faces were stuck in a pose looking like they'd seen a ghost, because they couldn't believe he showed up.

Cousin Aretha is the traveler. She's traveled the world and eager to tell where she's been and what she plans to do. Cousin Arethas got non-stop stories to tell, and she feels more like a stranger than family. She's traveled so much the only way she relates to others is through telling her stories from traveling abroad.

Aunt Pearl is the hypochondriac and is always complaining. She has top notch Academy Award winning sick-acting skills. No matter how hard you try to escape her presence — like a plague is coming— she wants to tell everyone what medications she takes; tell you about every doctor she can think of and you've never heard of… Aunt Pearl's tried every new diet and home health remedy and wants everyone to try her latest one as soon as we get home.

You can never seem to escape the family member who never stops talking. We try not to be rude to Uncle Earl, but keeping our eyelids open is a challenge. Uncle Earl could probably talk non-stop for DAYS — to a tree. It's like OH-MY-GOD-DO-THEY-EVER-STOP-TALKING! Wait! Does he even know what he is saying? By the time the day is over we can't remember what the hell he was talking about.

Now back to Aunt Pearl again. God bless her, because she's been slipping on some of the recipes she's known to cook well. Everyone is trying to be nice, but frowning and running away from the food once they find out she's cooked it.

And last but not least we can't forget the many family members who come with nothing and leave with massive quantities of everything cooked during the holiday. It's like you see them, and now you don't. They've escaped with the last piece of pound cake and the rest of the good food is packed up and gone.

I know, I'm writing about the good bad and ugly and maybe some things should not be said. Even though the things I mentioned maybe embarrassing and strange I love the people who gave me this story – my family. They are part of the fabric of my life. I am grateful. I wouldn't have it any other way. I need and want my family. I need those who love me. They are important and matter to me. Family is powerful and priceless. Family is everything and the holidays help keep me from forgetting…

Religion

I don't like when people ask me, "What church do you go to and what's your religion?" *Loaded questions.* After someone asks me these questions their facial expression tells me they are carefully calculating how I might respond. I know, if I don't answer the way they predict I'll get a *'sinner going to hell'* look. In the past, I'd give my (conditioned) response like a zombie on autopilot. In a monotone voice, I'd explain, "My mother is Methodist and my father is Baptist. My brother and I attended Catholic school because a Christian education is the best education." Afterwards the other person looks confused and stares at me like I overloaded them with too much information. I probably should have kept my answers to myself. They probably wanted a simple answer or they wanted to put me in a red box, but I gave them a rainbow box. Afterwards, I felt like I should've just given them a shorter answer. Then my strong inner sistah girl voice speaks, "You don't have to give any answer because this is your journey!"

Religion can be a touchy subject because everyone experiences the world differently. Sometimes we can hold onto religious dogma a little too tight. I'll explain…

I turned the car into the driveway and glanced over to see my next door neighbor watching her kids playing in their yard. I parked, got out of the van, unbuckled my two kids, and walked over to greet her and her kids. My daughter stood by my side. I held my son in my arms. I said, "Hello!" We began talking about our kids and how they grow so fast. I remember Halloween is two weeks away and I say, "What will your kids dress up as for Halloween this year?" She affirmed, "We don't do Halloween. It's a pagan celebration!" *I stood there and thought what does that mean and why did she answer with such fear?* People back in the day celebrated Halloween like those in Mexico celebrate the day of the dead; remembering those we love who have died and pasted on to the spirit world. Halloween though it's had different references in the past is also a time to celebrate the transition of from fall to winter. *When did Halloween become fun for some and fearful for others?* She made me feel like I committed a crime for asking a simple question. What's the worst that can happen letting kids play dress up for one day and eat candy under parent supervision? What? Is Jesus Christ going physically land in front of her house and blow it up if she doesn't follow an ancient myth. The conversation ended with goodbyes and the kids starring at each other like all they wanted to do is play. An awkward moment getting even more awkward because two days later the doorbell rings and I open the door. The same neighbor stands at my door with a paper in her hand. She says, "I want to give you this information as to why Halloween is bad!" I grabbed the sheet of paper and said, "Thank you !" I closed the door. I read the pamphlet, but the information is not new to me. Really — is it that serious?

Then there are others who express their religious beliefs openly. On social media my faithful brothers and sisters talk about God through quoting and posting bible verse after bible verse after bible verse like they are stuck in the same vibration of quoting bible verses. There is a difference between doing and being.

I observe people who distort the bible to fit

everything *everybody else* is doing *wrong*. To them the bible, which is a wonderful book, represents all there is, in our multiverse. There is so much more to learn when we learn to allow.

Religion can be defined as the ego's attempt to put spirituality in a box with a stack of rules. I relate more to the meaning of the word spirituality than the meaning of the word religion. Through my filter of experiences, spirituality has many definitions but, a simple one is the journey of understanding ones' own personal truth by rediscovering the love within. Religion and most things stemming from it was created to help us understand spirituality through the teachings of others, to get us back to who we are and our purpose here on earth.

Today, I don't declare myself as being part of any organized religious group, however, I am open to learning. Some of us need religion to help us create who we want to be. When we confine ourselves to one experience it's like shutting the door on many worlds. I am not defined by a series of dogma and rules. I don't think God would want me to restrict myself to the beauty and love we created together.

Love is the center of most religions or beliefs. Love is infinite. You cannot create or destroy it. Love. It is the most powerful. You can be on your death bed and the love of family and friends can turn death into life. Love can grab you from the depths of the cycle of your own hell. Love can hit you so hard you won't even know your name. Love is everything and can mean multiple things. It's who we are and meant to be. It's what we are meant to give to each other.

We all have the opportunity to live their own journey. When we jump out of and into someone else's lane on the many freeways of love, is when problems are created.

So the next time someone asks me what my religion is I don't know what I will say, or if I will have the courage to step out on a limb and say I have no religion. I don't know, if I will say nothing at all, or if I will say Love. One thing I do know; this is my journey!

Life

I don't want to die. I have so many things I want to do, but fear seeps in every crack of my heart like water fills the cracks of the dry dessert ground. Thinking about it causes me to feel overwhelmed. I want to grow old and live like my Aunt Mae who died at ninety seven years old.

I was 12-years-old when our next door neighbor Mrs. Collard died. A great woman who meant a lot to my family. Mrs. Collard was more like family than a friend. She kept my brother during my birth and could make the best gumbo. For Halloween she gave fruit instead of candy. Her house always felt clean and all her furniture immaculately placed. A kind and gentle woman I won't forget.

My mother wanted to go to Mrs. Collards funeral, but knew ahead of time she wouldn't be able to go. So, my mother decided to go to the viewing. I remember being scared to go, because I could feel Mommas fear and hesitation. At this point in my life I had attended one funeral, but had no memory of it. Mrs. Collard would be my first time remembering and seeing a dead body.

The day of the viewing my mother and I walked in the building holding hands like we'd seen a ghost and only in the lobby of the mortuary. We signed in and one of the funeral people told us where to go see our neighbor. As we were walking to the chapel I could feel the anxiety build up in my chest. My hands and feet started to get cold and sweaty. All kinds of questions came into my mind. *What will she look like? Will I recognize her? I wonder what her body would feel like if I touch it? I hope the body doesn't move while I'm here. Why am I so scared? How can people work here, around dead bodies?*

As soon as we walked in the room where her casket laid, I could feel love, calm and peace. Her body lay in state. She had her rosary beads in her hands. She had on a light pink gown. She glowed. My mother and I kneeled down and looked her over. My mother and I agreed (without words) she looked great. We left feeling better than when we came and glad we attended.

Today, I am still learning to let go of my death fear and allow. Death is one of those things still haunting me even though I know more and have a little more experience under my belt. But, it is hard. Today it's been two years since the death of my father and the memory brought the fear back home to my heart and has made me even more curious about the death process. *What happens when you die? What happens after you die? What happens when you reach the other side and who is there? Do people look the same and are they in the same body?* The more questions, the more I discover the fear of dying is more powerful than dying. *I'm alive and haven't died, but that's my guess.*

Why can't death be more of a celebration and not this depressingly sad event? Why are we so consumed with it on TV and why has my condition taught me fear? Why don't we embrace it? Why don't we talk about it? All questions I may never get an answer to.

During Daddy's funeral I felt like I watched everything as it unfolded before me (like an outer body experience). Some of my family members were so dramatic, and others overcome with grief. I grieved months before his death and now I think it may have been years. I cried for my father, for years, because I held onto his pain. Pain not belonging to me. When he died his pain became his again and I let go. When I saw his body the first time I was scared as hell, but I could feel that Daddy was just fine and somewhere on another journey, *in this life*, I cannot understand. He is with me in a new way. He is always here in spirit when I call him. He is my angel.

Funerals are for the living and death is a reminder of how precious life is and how it should be lived. Death is really the fear of letting go of what is not natural causing pain in our life. Every moment we have fear we are dying and loosing precious time on earth. Death teaches me to live my life loving others, to be present to each moment, create more fun for myself, being kind to others, and grateful for each moment.

Just Be

I just got slapped with information I understand in a different way. It took a long time, but now I see, because the light is finally on... I'm so excited and I don't know why I couldn't see or understand it before now. I've been worrying and thinking and now it's almost funny recalling my struggle with the words *'Just Be'* and my search for its meaning in my life. I sat and wondered how am I supposed to *'Just Be'*, but the more I wondered, I realized, I was just wondering instead of being. All I need to do is, 'Just Be'. I feel like the secret code is cracked, even though many people throughout my life have said, "Be yourself!", which is another way of saying just be. *Why did I make it so complicated?* I guess my mind had to think, analyze and manipulate the information before I could accept changing my way of thinking.

In a video on YouTube a man explained it perfectly. He said, "We are human beings, not human becoming's." Afterwards, I laughed out loud. In other words, stop thinking about what you want to become, be who you are becoming. It's so simple and true. Just be means doing what makes us happy or finding the good in what we have already in this moment. So if you want to be a writer, then write. Just be a writer. Sign up for a class or volunteer to write stories for a community magazine. If you want to go back to school make an appointment with a counselor and plan the steps to get back in school. Don't just talk about it and watch the dream float away passing you by day after day. If you want to teach volunteer at a school and talk to teachers to find out what they did to get to where they are. If you want to paint go to the store right now and get some paint and start painting. If there is something you want to do, do it. Get the ball rolling being who you want to be and before you know it you'll have become what you dreamed of becoming.

Take a step, Just Be yourself!

I Believe

I believe in God,
the Father Almighty,
Creator of Heaven and earth.
I believe in Jesus Christ, His only Son, our Lord,
who was conceived by the Holy Spirit,
born of the Virgin Mary,
suffered under Pontius Pilate,
was crucified, died and was buried.
He descended to the dead.
On the third day, He rose again.
He ascended to Heaven and is seated at the right
hand of the Father.
He will come again to judge the living and the
dead.

I believe in the Holy Spirit,
the Holy Catholic Church,
the communion of saints,
the forgiveness of sins,
the resurrection of the body,
and life everlasting. Amen.

Do you remember reciting these words in church? It's the Apostle's Creed. For some of us this is a well-known prayer. I remember reciting a slightly different version as a child, in the Methodist church, with my Mom. The prayer could be found in the back of the dark red hymnal for those of us who didn't have it memorized. The Apostle's Creed is usually recited before communion on the first Sunday of every month, before receiving the body and blood of Christ which is expressed by partaking bread and drinking good ole grape juice, as a kid, I always wanted more of… I don't remember reciting the same prayer in the Baptist church with my Daddy but, I'm sure there is another version, I didn't know about, which meant the same. Whatever the differences, reciting the prayer affirmed what I believed, at one time in my life. The prayer gave me the tools I needed to be who I am today.

As I am reminiscing about prayers, affirmations and church I feel something deep within. I know it's time again to affirm out loud, and write down for my own reference what I believe. What do I believe? What do I believe now since my perspective on life is different from many years ago? What do I believe because, I don't hold firmly onto many religious practices with a firm grip? What do I believe now since I am learning how to allow myself to be present to life? What do I believe now because I want love and peace to filter my experiences? What do I believe now because I know there is no certain way to be? What do I believe now since I have awakened to more of my own truth?

I believe God is love.

I believe human language cannot fully describe or capture the power of God, All or One.

I believe we are each an expression of the same God-energy and are meant to have different experiences to learn about who we are.

I believe God is not something living outside of our self. God flows through us.

I believe if we are present to the energy of God we can see mirrors of ourselves in each other and get answers to the most pressing questions we have on our journey.

I believe our Spirit is eternal. Our love ones and

ancestors who've passed on continue to love us and watch over us even when we don't fully understand how the Spirit of God works.

I believe we heal when we give love to each other.

I believe we are all students and teachers for each other. We learn how to be better students when we teach and we learn how to be better teachers when we are students.

I believe we feel our part of God in the stillness within our self.

I believe we are on God's time and we must do the very best we can to love as much as we can.

I believe everything happens in cycles. If we are too hard-headed to learn a lesson that lesson will keep showing itself to us over and over until we allow the experience to unfold as it should.

I believe we can create whatever we want if we are patient and present to the flow of life.

I believe our conditions of the past do not define who we are in this moment.

I believe we each have a piece of greatness we have to learn how to uncover.

I believe what I say is not new or different. Many

healers (Jesus, Buddha) have tried to teach us.

I believe as I evolve, parts of my beliefs, will change and more will be added.

Resisting

I've resisted all these years. Knowing, but not knowing. Doing, but, not knowing I'm doing. The plan is already set in stone; I refused to see it. The ground shifted beneath me, and I didn't know it. All I had to do is jump in the river and let it lead me, but I wanted to stay behind, and stand on the river banks and watch the river flow past me. I wanted the veil to cover my eyes and continue to give me blurry vision, because I didn't want to deal with it. I fought against it, but today my hands are up and I surrender because now it wins.

Throughout my life people would say you should be a teacher, you should be some kind of leader, you should hold a major job position like it is expected of me. I wonder why people on my journey would pause and just listen to me. Their focus and silence while I spoke startled me, at times, because they listened intently like time stopped. Maybe I am the only one who could hear their spirit yearning for a loving message.

I have a hard time with the attention, because I prefer staying behind the scenes in most situations. A friend of mine said to me, "You are not a wallflower!" *Okay! Wow!* But those words bothered me. Those words hurt a little. The phrase echoed in my mind, like he said it in a James Earl Jones voice. Finally, I googled the word wallflower and it says: *someone with an introverted personality type who socially are competent enough to be liked and to attend group gatherings, but may choose or feel the need to blend in and remain silent. Why am I giving this word wallflower so much power?* Ten minutes have pass and I'm now reading the definition a few more times. I'm letting someone else's definition of who they think I am get me sidetracked. I know who I created myself to be, but deep within me something is screaming at me to wake up and allow. When you spend a lot of time on something and you don't know why, it's time to look at it further. I mean go for a walk or do what you do to feel and understand what's happening. I don't like what he said, but maybe my

---

friend is right. I am not a wallflower. I'm a leader, I have always been; it comes natural.

Now, I don't have a clue about where to go from here, but I know leading means different things. Leading is intimidating and I don't want to be in a situation where the blind leads the blind. Leading is hard, because in some situations it could seem like the world is on my shoulders. I'm starting to make excuses for what already is and excuses are walls of fear. I've been a leader before and I've been leading all this time. The awareness and acceptance is what's different.

All I can do is be me within my truth and within my journey. All I can do is love myself and inspire others to love themselves. We are all leaders leading the way so light can shine for others who are in the dark searching for their own light switch.

ONE

"Digital media creates visual messages so powerful it changes how billions of people think and believe. Subliminally feeding our subconscious while we think we are conscious of what we are experiencing. Corporations and politicians know this game and take advantage any chance they get. They understand common awareness. They know the fearful unconsciously feed off of messages like a rabid dog in the wild eating a dead carcass after weeks without food. They know we hunger for the same and they'll keep feeding us into a trance like thinking until they get bored." - Allura Eshmun 2015

We go through great lengths to understand our self, outside our self, because deep down we long for within our self, and not getting enough from outside of our self. We can only learn when we are being and creating who we want to be. We have been evolving into new lives helping us to expand and do what we are wanting.

Over the years, I watched groups of animals; a herd of cows, a flock of birds and a group of ants. I always wondered and fascinated by how, why and what makes each group do the same thing? How do all the birds know to fly south for the winter? How do ants know what job they are supposed to have in the ant colony? Then I thought group consciousness; shared or common awareness unifying a group. They know, only the same. For humans, what we create seems different until we understand we are creating contrasts of the same. Our experiences leading us towards understanding this is different, but we travel the same human path to get to where we are going. Animals know what they are created to do and they do it, because of common awareness. Humans have the same common awareness, but our ego complicates things. Ego gives us full experiences. It helps us mediate through our emotions. As I thought about it more we are like ants we are all the same it's just the mind eludes us into thinking we are different and separate from each other. The mind is doing what it's meant to do.

We separate ourselves, by putting God outside ourselves and into a box with rules. We created it to be called religion. When really there is no God. Not in the way our condition and religious teachings pound into our heads. God is not an entity outside of us, or up in the clouds, or in a statue or picture or in a book. Those things are items, tools, guides reminders of God. God is the energy flowing through all of us giving us life. Everything has a piece of God-energy.

We are the human experience of God living on earth. Breathe. The breath we take every moment of our lives is the life of God. Each breathe gives us opportunity to enjoy the beauty of the human journey. God is the consciousness connecting us on this planet earth; together this power makes us One. We are all the same.

All the excess thinking we do causes us to separate ourselves from each other and against our true nature creating fear. We have the power to change by giving and receiving love to each other. When we are full of love the faster we experience the abundance of life and our experiences. Those of us who meditate, pray, and who are mindful have learned to tap into this truth.

Religion or spirituality which the mind or thinking created gets us back to part of the God-energy living in all things. Going to church and having something to believe in raises our vibration or God-energy and makes us feel good to know we belong and are a part of something bigger than the human experience. In part, we are longing for the same. That's why so many of us follow and cling onto religious rituals. It's where we are most comfortable. We are one who created many through many journeys and we will slowly find our way home to one again.

A sneak peek at Allura Eshmun's new book coming soon!!!

Insane Scavenger Hunt:

You are not Crazy, Just Awakening!

1. QUESTIONS ROAMING IN MY MIND

"I am roaming aimlessly in my own mind today." - liona V.

For 3-years during my late 30's, I questioned my life. I questioned the past, present and tried to envision the future. All the thoughts and feelings arising from the questioning slowly depressed and confused me. I felt lost; so, I prayed. I prayed long and hard, for days, to make the uncomfortable emotions stop; not totally understanding my feelings and what is happening to me. So many days passed before I realized I prayed for hours almost every night. For weeks, I woke up in the mornings feeling tired and burdened by the same questions. My mind wandered; traveling from story to story and scenario after scenario. I read spiritual books, Every day I Pray or Until Today by Iyanla Vanzant, hoping to receive the encouragement needed to focus my thoughts into a positive direction. I felt like maybe, I needed to change my attitude by just being happy. So I faked it until I made it just like the saying says, but the questions continued. I desperately looked for something, anything, but not sure what to look for. I felt like I searched in the dark but, my eyes were open in bright daylight. Then I thought maybe I needed to catch-up with God and if I caught up then my life would improve and be okay. I picked up my Bible then put it down, thinking, I don't even understand all these words and what they mean and how these Bible stories are relevant to my life. I began feeling guilty about not going to church on a regular basis. Then all of a sudden my questions stop and I began to daydream. I heard the words in my mind,

PRAISE THE LORD, AMEN, HALLELUJAH! Those familiar words take me back to my   8-year-old-self sitting and watching the folks of Saint Paul Methodist Church.

[I'm sitting between Momma and Mother (my grandmother) on an uncomfortable wooden pew trying to stay awake as the reverend preaches his

sermon. Reverend Bell is excited and feeling the Spirit because he is almost singing his words and constantly wiping the sweat from his forehead as he talks to the congregation. The piano player just sat back down, put his hands on the keys and starts to play 2 chords every time the Reverend ends a sentence.

Wearing your Sunday best is serious business. I see the ladies witnessing the spirit of the Lord with their arms up and I hear their amens and yes pastor. They are wearing flamboyant hats with matching suits, shoes and purse. I straighten out my pretty pink dress and tug my white socks with lace ruffles. My hair is cute because Momma hot combed my hair last night. My naturally tight curly coiled hair is slick, straight and greased down with Royal Crown hair dressing; into two pony tails platted on the ends. I know I look good because my patent leather shoes match my patent leather purse just like Momma and Mother.

Several minutes later Reverend begins preaching louder and clearly but, my mind is more concerned about my empty growling stomach and I can't wait to take off these cute hot and itchy clothes. I wonder what my brother Lee is doing at the Zion Baptist church with Daddy.

My boredom starts to fade because Reverend Bell stopped preaching. The choir stood to sing, Hush, Somebody's Calling My Name, but I know it's going to be at least an hour before church is over.]

Back to the current moment; the questions and thoughts came back and I remember the words of my late grandmother echo in my head like a broken record on a continuous loop. She'd say, "Allura you need to put them kids in church," but, at the same time, I know, I don't fit in at church and church these days seems more of a place of entertainment and not a sacred place or space for worship. I want my kids to have the church experience, but feel no urgency to go because church has too many rules and judges. *What's with all the restrictions anyway?* I mean, really, who wants to sit on a hard bench pew for two-and-a-half hours next to two children who are, bored out of their minds and hungry because they are used-to-having-lunch-right-now, and a husband who would rather be home relaxing. *Do we really need to sing five different hymns and all three verses sung in a slow, southern, Negro spiritual drawl? Did I mention acapella?* For me, trying to stay respectfully awake and listening to a minister struggling to make the words of the Bible relevant to today's problems is challenging! It's natural for me to feel this way. Right?

What is this thing that's driving me nuts? Why do I feel guilty? I need to try harder because if I try harder things will work much better for me. I am a college-educated-women with tons of experience and skills. Why am I not able to get the job, and money I want? What am I doing wrong? This is driving me crazy. Why am I so consumed with all of these questions? My life is not bad. Why are all these women with extreme low self-esteem issues coming in and out of my life? Why am I so worried about them and why do I feel so bad after they leave my life? Why am I complaining about nothing? I shouldn't complain. I have everything. Why am I not satisfied? I have my own life right? God, are you listening? Are you out there? If you are in everything, surely you can hear me screaming in my prayers. Is it something you want me to learn? Help? What the hell is it? And why don't I have any real friends? Maybe, I need to diversify friendships. I need some gay friends. Those with the title "friend" all need some kinda help and it's as if they're all reaching out to me for something and I don't know how to give it to them 'cause I don't know what it is? I'm not perfect. Who am I to help them? I need help. We all have issues. They all have issues; as do I but, they only come around or call when they need some.....*

Go to AlluraEshmun.com for release date of Insane Scavenger Hunt: You're Not Crazy Just Awakening!

www.ingramcontent.com/pod-product-compliance
Lightning Source LLC
Chambersburg PA
CBHW021131020426
42331CB00005B/721